Understanding My Attention-Deficit/ Hyperactivity Disorder

by Kara T. Tamanini, M.S., LMHC

Eloquent Books

New York, New York

Eloquent Books
An imprint of AEG Publishing Group
845 Third Avenue, 6th Floor – 6016
New York, NY 10022
www.eloquentbooks.com

ISBN: 978-1-60693-170-7   1-60693-170-9

Printed in the United States of America

For my wonderful husband, Keith, and my
daughter, Kaley.

With special thanks to my parents who have
supported me every step of the way
and to my brother, Craig, thanks for your help
with this project.

Love,
Kara T.

This story is about a boy named Tommy who is having trouble at home and school. This tale is to help children and adults understand the symptoms of

Attention-Deficit/Hyperactivity Disorder

and how it affects them.

This is a story about poor Tommy Davis who was always in trouble. Tommy has been sad since he started kindergarten and thinks that nobody likes him anymore.

He sits sadly in the store while his mother and little sister shop for a new toy for his sister Amy.

Tommy looks up and sees the store owner, Mr. Timmons, standing over him. "It's good to see you again Tommy, is something wrong?" asks Mr. Timmons. "Why are you sitting here looking so very sad while you are in my toy store?

"I am not getting a toy, because I am always in trouble at home and at school," he says to Mr. Timmons. "I don't understand why I can't be good, no matter what I do."

"I have been in trouble every day at school for not sitting still in my chair and not listening to my teacher. The teacher gets mad when I don't raise my hand and yell out the answers. Yesterday, I had to go to the principal's office because I have been in trouble so many times with my teacher, Ms. Lincoln. I just can't help it."

Mr. Timmons looked at Tommy and said, "Tommy, lots of little kids have trouble paying attention and listening at school. Don't worry, nothing is as bad as it seems."

"But all the kids make fun of me when I get in trouble, and that hurts my feelings," Tommy exclaims.

"I want to tell you a story about a little boy I knew who was ALWAYS in trouble. Listen carefully, okay?" says Mr. Timmons.

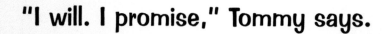

"I will. I promise," Tommy says.

"I knew a little boy who lived near here and he was around your age. In the morning, he never wanted to get out of bed because he was always in trouble. His mom and dad were always yelling at him because he never seemed to listen to them and they had to tell him the same thing over and over again before he heard them," Mr. Timmons says.

"This little boy never wanted to go to school because the teacher was always fussing at him for getting up out of his chair and bothering the other kids in class. He always had problems sleeping at night and in the morning he was sooo tired."

"Wow!" Tommy shouts. "The boy sounds like he was really BAD."

"No, not really Tommy, but let me go on with my story," Mr. Timmons says.

"He would forget his homework in the morning when he went to school. Then he would end up getting a bad grade, because he had left his homework or his backpack in his bedroom."

"He always asked to get out of his seat and get something to drink or to go to the bathroom so he would not have to stay in his chair."

"You know what else?" Sometimes he would just sit there all day staring out the window and not do any of his school work and he had to repeat a grade because his grades were sooo very bad," Mr. Timmons explained.

"Wow, Mr. Timmons, this kid sure was not doing well in school, was he?" asks Tommy.

"No, Tommy he wasn't doing well at all," says Mr. Timmons. "In fact, he was angry a lot of the time and he would hit the other kids in school when he got really mad."

"It got so bad that the principal started calling his parents at home and telling them how bad the little boy had acted at school."

Tommy interrupted and asked, "Mr. Timmons, did the little boy in your story ever get OUT of trouble?"

"Wait a minute Tommy, let me finish my story."
"The boy in my story also had trouble with INTERRUPTING others when they were talking and he never seemed to wait his turn and butted in line."

"He did not have many friends at school and the other kids made fun of him because he talked all the time. They called him a TROUBLE MAKER!!!"

"Everyone said he never seemed to listen and do what he was told."

Tommy's mother walks up and starts talking to Mr. Timmons. "Good to see you again Mr. Timmons, how are you today?" I saw you over here talking to Tommy. What are you two talking about for so long?"

"Hi, Mrs. Davis, I am telling your son a story about a little boy I once knew, and I am almost done with the story," says Mr. Timmons.

"Okay, Mr. Timmons, we are almost done shopping and we will be back in a few minutes," Tommy's mother says.

"As I was saying, everyone thought this little boy was being bad on purpose," Mr. Timmons says.

"So what happened next Mr. Timmons?"
Tommy asks.

"The little boy's mother got so concerned about how he was acting and that his grades were so bad that his mother went and saw his teacher at school. She ended up taking him to the doctor to see what was wrong. She found out from the doctor that he indeed did have a problem concentrating and paying attention and he wasn't being bad on purpose.

"After the boy got help, he started doing much better in school and was able to sit still and listen when the teacher was talking and his grades got a lot better.

"He also began making friends because he wasn't in trouble all the time, and he was MUCH happier."

Mr. Timmons stood up to leave and said, "Tommy, it has been really nice talking to you, but I have to get back to work."

As Mr. Timmons was about to leave, Tommy's mother and sister came around the corner. "Are you two done talking?" Tommy's mother asks.

"Yes mom we are and he told me a story about a boy just like me," Tommy says excitedly.

"Tommy, that story about the little boy was actually about me when I was about your age," Mr. Timmons says. "I told your mom that story a few days ago when she was here in the toy store. She told me how much trouble you have been having at school."

"Everybody has problems at one time or another, but you just need somebody to help you," Mr. Timmons says. "You have to believe that things can get better and think that you can achieve anything, but it also takes a lot of work on your part, too."

"I don't feel as sad now after hearing your story," says Tommy.

"Would you like to go to the playground on the way home then Tommy?" asks Tommy's mother.

"Yes, let's go, I love the playground!" exclaims Tommy.

"Goodbye Mr. Timmons. Thanks for telling me your story," Tommy says.

"You're welcome Tommy and I wish you the best," says Mr. Timmons.

"Tommy and I will let you know about his progress in school," says Tommy's mother, "Thanks for sharing your story with him."

Tommy smiles as he runs from the toy store to go to the playground with his mom and sister.

Tommy is having difficulty at home and at school focusing his attention, listening in class, completing his assignments and is doing poorly in school. He also has trouble sitting still, keeping his hands to himself, waiting his turn, and staying in his seat. Tommy is exhibiting symptoms of

Attention-Deficit/Hyperactivity Disorder and a health care professional should be consulted to determine a course of treatment if needed. ADHD is a common disorder seen in children and the purpose of this book is to bring awareness and understanding to this particular disorder and is not intended to diagnose or to treat ADHD.